Presented to New
covenant Baptist
church by

W P Lay

Pathways to
A Wonderful Life

Christian Poetry

WILLIS PAUL LAY

WESTBOW·
PRESS
A DIVISION OF THOMAS NELSON
& ZONDERVAN

Scripture taken from the King James Version of the Bible.

WestBow Press books may be ordered through booksellers or by contacting:

WestBow Press
A Division of Thomas Nelson & Zondervan
1663 Liberty Drive
Bloomington, IN 47403
www.westbowpress.com
1 (866) 928-1240

ISBN: 978-1-4908-3623-2 (sc)
ISBN: 978-1-4908-3624-9 (e)

Library of Congress Control Number: 2014907921

Printed in the United States of America.

WestBow Press rev. date: 6/30/2014

Dedication

*This book is dedicated to everyone who has
encouraged me to continue writing poems and put
them in print. I especially would like to mention
Ron Sierra who first told me to write a book. I
would also like to mention George Cook and
Roosevelt Lovelace who also encouraged me before
I retired at the Post Office. I would also like to
dedicate it to my wife Pat for patiently allowing
me to work on this book without complaining.*

Contents

I will sing unto the Lord as long as I live
Psalm 104:33

A Wonderful Life

We often dream of having
a wonderful life
Where there'll be no quarrels,
Struggles or strife

But, this world isn't perfect
No, not in the least little bit
But, let's not begin to panic
Or pitch a fit

Instead let's try to change
Our world each day
Yes, let's try to make a difference
In every way

Therefore, let's seek God's help
As we face each day
Yes, let's let him guide and direct us
Along our way

Then we'll begin to see and feel
A wonderful life
Even tho the world has its quarrels,
Struggles and strife

*From the rising of the sun unto the going down
of the same the Lord's name is to be praised
Psalm 113:3*

A Beautiful Sunset

*God has so many things that are beautiful. We
don't always take the time to stop and see the beauty
around us.*

*How many sunsets have you stopped to watch? I
know I have missed quite a few. One day a last sunset
we will see, for our lives on this earth will end. But God,
heaven and an eternal day with no darkness await those
who love him and his son Jesus.*

*Ask someone to join you in watching a beautiful
sunset.*

The Sun

*The sun seems to slip away
without any warning day by day*

*It first slips up and then it slips down
for the earth just keeps on spinning around*

*Beautiful and majestic in every way
it puts light from its creator on display*

*From sunrise to sunset,
light and warmth it will give
Oh, may we do likewise
through the life that we live*

A Beautiful Sunset

A beautiful sunset I see God showing
and though I bid it to stay,
it longs to be going

God hang the sun way up in the sky
now I'm watching it wave goodbye

It's so big and the clouds are so pink
it seems to hover, as it gets ready to sink

The birds are resting out on a limb
The light is fading and it soon will be dim

One day a last sunset I will see
Oh! Let me not worry while there's breath in me

For God has promised
me a home in heaven one day
Where all darkness and fear
will have all fled away

Sweet Bread Recipe

Whether it's making some tasty bread or working
In the garden it's going to take some effort on our part.
Too many marriages are ending up in divorce. Let's
Work to keep our marriages healthy. Let's let our lives
Be sprinkled with fun and excitement!

As The Marriage Begins

God gives us a mate
It's - - - until death do us part
and as the marriage begins
there's usually love in each heart

But, like a beautiful garden
that needs someone's care each day
There's need to till the soil
and pull all the weeds away

Weeds of unforgiveness
Weeds of bitterness and strife
Weeds of anger and contention
Often spring up in one's life

So let's pull them up
and burn them each day
Then after the smoke rises
love and kindness will be on the way

4

*Let the husband render unto the
wife due benevolence;
and likewise also the wife unto the husband.
1 Corinthians 7:3*

Sweet Bread Recipe

*Let faithful wives begin
by baking some sweet bread
For this recipe that prevents strife
husbands often need to be fed*

*And they'll be quite hungry
for your special today
So mix your ingredients in the proper way*

*You'll also need to have a large bowl
to mix in all the good ingredients
for your husbands hungry soul*

*Just mix in peace, love and virtue as you begin
Then toss in kindness and praise
while stirring at the end*

*As the oven gets ready,
place your ingredients in the pan
and after the bread cooks,
serve with sugar to your hungry man*

Whoso findeth a wife findeth a good thing, and obtaineth favor of the Lord. Proverbs18:22

I Love You

*I had just began to write poems when my wife said,
"Honey, why don't you write me
a poem?" So this is how
it turned out.
I thank God for my wife. She has been faithful in
many ways. We have walked side
by side for many years.*

My Faithful Wife

*If I glance back in time there's quite a bit to see
My faithful wife, always walking beside of me*

*Taking care of the children
Preparing all the meals
Washing the clothes
Shopping for the good deals*

*When I got very sick, she was always there
Praying to the Lord while I was in her care*

*If I glance forward in time
what do I hope to see
My faithful wife,
always walking beside of me*

I Love You

Just a little poem to you my dear wife
To let you know I love you,
And thank God you share my life

When we met on that wonderful day
It was God that arranged it,
To help us on our way

For after we met we soon said, "I do"
We then got our first home,
It was just me and you

But then the children came along
And we were both filled with pride
And like a mother hen,
Under your wings they did hide

As the years went by, and the children moved away
Through my sickness and health,
You were there to stay

And if I had to do it all over once again
To more often say, "I love you"
Would surely be my plan

Mama

It was hard to let mama go. Her kidneys failed and she went on dialysis. She kept losing weight and the dialysis seemed to take all of her strength.

But her faith in the Lord Jesus continued to remain strong throughout her illness and as her health continued to fail we were with her when she went on to be with Jesus.

Forevermore

We were with mama
as she came to death's door
and when she went through,
we were saddened - - - forevermore

But she traveled on to a very peaceful shore
To meet with many loved ones,
and be with Jesus - - - forevermore

And now she is waiting,
yes, near heavens door
where we'll soon be together,
with her - - - forevermore

Despise not thy mother when she is old
Proverbs 23:22

Mama

Mama how we miss you,
now that you're gone
But heaven couldn't wait
and now we feel so alone

We still remember the sparkle in your eyes
and we were so sad
as we said our last goodbyes

But now you're in heaven
with the heavenly bands
singing praises to Jesus with uplifted hands

We also remember what you used to say,
"Put your trust in Jesus
for he's the only way"

Therefore I believe you often
go near heavens gate
and pray we'll trust the Lord
before it becomes too late

But if the Spirit of him that raised Jesus from the dead dwell in you, he that raised up Christ from the dead shall also quicken your mortal bodies by his Spirit that dwelleth in you. Romans 8:11

Is God Too Big

I believe God is everywhere his creation exists as his servant David says in Psalm 139, yet he is also inside each believer who trusts in him. (Romans 8:11) This comes into perspective when we consider the great truth that God is a Trinity. (Father, Son and Holy Spirit)

Never Be Small

When I look at the stars on a clear and cloudless night
When I look at the moon so full and so very bright

When I see and feel the sun on a
clear and cloudless day
Then I begin to feel very small and
so then I begin to pray

"Who am I Lord that thou should consider me
and why for ever creature Lord
was Jesus nailed to Calvary's tree"

Then God whispers back
"Those who respond to my loving call
will be filled with my Holy Spirit
and shall never be small"

*7 Whither shall I go from thy spirit? Or whither shall
I flee from thy presence?
8 If I ascend up into heaven, thou
art there; if I make my
bed in hell, behold, thou art there. Psalm 139:7-8*

Is God Too Big

*Is god too big for my little eyes to behold
For when he spoke the word
great galaxies began to unfold
And when he spread his mighty wings,
did not heaven and earth begin to sing
Therefore when he came into my heart,
was it a small thing
For now I can feel the great depth
of his love and marvelous grace
and now I experience his great pardon,
Because Jesus suffered and died in my place
And I stand utterly amazed
at how much my little faith has grown
For I can now see a holy God
sitting upon his heavenly throne
And near his right hand
stands a lamb once slain for you and me
Oh! Jesus is his name
begin to let the vision set you free*

Forgive

As we go through life we will be offended and hurt by other people many times. Christ taught forgiveness of sins and if someone sincerely asks us to forgive them shouldn't we? It will take God's help but let's ask him for power to forgive others.

Seventy Times Seven

"Seventy times seven,"
the Lord told Peter to forgive
Christ's life was an example
of how we should live

While dying on the cross
he chose not to blame
Asking his father to forgive them
Oh! Can't we do the same

Therefore let's take forgiveness
from our treasure chest
then give it to others,
that Christ may be blessed

We only have one life to live,
Therefore let it be said,
we know how to forgive

Judge not, and ye shall not be judged; condemn not, and ye shall not be condemned; forgive, and ye shall be forgiven; St. Luke 6:37

Forgive

Sometimes we get hurt and don't want to forgive
Bitterness comes into our heart
and it's no life to live

So as we go down life's road
and search for what is best
If we take our problems to the Lord
we will soon find sweet rest

For when we talk to Jesus
and ask him what to do
He'll ask us to forgive others
just as he has forgiven me and you

Maybe it's a loved one,
or a neighbor next door,
who needs us to forgive them
and love them evermore

So let's not think being bitter is best
for it will soon destroy us,
along with our rest

Remember Jesus is waiting and watching
to see what we will do
So let's not disappoint him,
for he has forgiven me and you

Wearing A Mask

Are we real or do we wear a mask? We should live out our lives without any secrecy or deception. In short our lives should be an open book for all to see.

An Open Book

Some folks are like an open book
There's no secrecy or deception
when we take a look

But other folks are different,
they tend to live on the sly
We often see hypocrisy as they live out a lie

All of our life events
are written down in God's great book
Where one day in the future
heaven will take a look

When Christ lived his life
it was like an open book
Millions are now changed
as they closely take a look

A hypocrite with his mouth destroyeth his neighbor; but through knowledge shall the just be delivered.

Proverbs 11:9

Wearing a Mask

*Are you real
or do you wear a mask
Is that really you
or should I dare to ask*

*We're all actors
on the great stage of life
Playing out our parts
in a world filled with strife*

*Oh! We may never commit murder
and stealing may not be our part
But do we possess either lust or greed
or is either pride or envy in our heart*

*The audience is watching
They often see what's deep within
As God reveals hidden secrets
and unmasks each and every sin*

*Oh! Is that really you
Oh! Let me dare to ask
Oh! Let me see your face
without your mask*

Keep thy tongue from evil, and thy lips from speaking guile. Psalm 34:13

When the Devil Hitches a Ride

Gossip, lies, envy, pride, half truths, rumors and
the list goes on. But how hurtful
these things can be. Let's
ask God to help us rid these things from our lives.

Blackberry Tea

Now that ole Devil is ornery
Yes, he's ornery as he can be
For I found him propped up at my table
drinking my - - - Blackberry Tea

He said though he's got many helpers
all over this great land
He just wanted to come by and invite folks
to play in his big ole band

Folks who could play a tune of gossip
or sing a song of lies were in demand
But if someone could toot a horn of envy and pride
they would be perfect for his band

When I told him I wasn't interested
he left as mad as he could be
Then I sat back down at my table
and had me some - - - Blackberry Tea

When the Devil Hitches a Ride

I went to church last Sunday
but soon found the Devil was there
He must have snuck in slyly
when we bowed our heads in prayer
He soon caused a lot of whispering
after some juicy gossip he began to spread
Seems the pastor and his sweet wife
were no longer sleeping in the same bed
Later on the Sunday school director
noticed two boys missing from Sunday school
Seems they had been quite busy
putting frogs in the baptismal pool
Later on the song leader's music
seemed to disappear in thin air
and as the pastor looked for his sermon notes,
well they just weren't there
When the church services finally ended
the Devil was still busy as a bee
telling everyone the latest gossip
then coming right up to me
He said he'd had a very nice time
and needed to hitch a ride
When I told him I was going the other way
he soon left with Mr. Pride
Now when the Devil comes to church
he almost always hitches a ride
and it's usually easy to spot him
for he sits next to Mr. Pride

The Potter

We may not like the idea of being a pot or vessel, but think how life would be without any pots or vessels to hold water, food and drinks. They are quite handy and useful when we need them.

God has chosen to work through us to tell the world about his son Jesus Christ. This is a great honor to all who will be a vessel in his mighty hand. He is the potter and we are the clay.

Earthen Vessels

We're all earthen vessels made by God's hands
And we are his children residing in so many lands

We carry the oil of his spirit
and the light of his son
The world is a mission field
where we introduce God's holy one

"Be filled with the Holy Spirit,"
is the message we share
for a life without Jesus,
oh, it's . . . empty and bare

But now, O Lord, thou art our father; we are the clay,
and thou our potter; and we are the work of thy hand.
Isaiah 64:8

The Potter

Lord, you are the potter and we are the clay
Mold us and make us in thy image we pray

And as we are turned,
on thy great potters wheel
may your truth, love and grace
be what our life will reveal

Also as thy gentle hands
give shape to each part
May your mercy and forgiveness
be revealed in our heart

Then as we are molded
into thy vessels of clay
May Christ be our example
that we follow each day

For a vessel of honor
we will all need to be
Filled with thy Holy Spirit
who cometh from thee

Laughter

After being in a bad mood for several days, my wife said, "Don't be so grumpy." Well I didn't think I was grumpy but I was. Let's get rid of the bad habit of griping and complaining.

Grumpy

*I looked at myself
and what did I see
Oh! There was a grumpy person
living inside of me*

*And all that Grumpy did
was gripe and complain
'Twas more than enough
to drive anyone insane*

*So while everyone was annoyed
I'm sure that God was annoyed too
by this grumpy person
who belonged in a zoo*

*So I told Grumpy to leave
and he left that very day
Then I gave a party
to celebrate his going away*

A merry heart doeth good like a medicine
Proverbs 17:22

Laughter

Is there laughter in your heart
or is your soul grumpy and need a jump start

Laughter is like a medicine
Yes, that's what they say
and this is one tonic that we need today

Not one grumpy person did God ever make
But we often get that way
when him we forsake

So Lord put laughter back into our hearts
Heal our land and give us a new start

Let us be like children who laugh and play
as they twist and turn and enjoy the day

Let grumpiness flee
Let our souls have sweet rest
May we smile and laugh and give you our best

*17 And he bearing his cross went forth into a place
Called the place of the skull, which is called in the
Hebrew Golgotha,
18 where they crucified him, and two others with him
On either side one, and Jesus in the midst.*

John 19:17-18

The Man I Met That Day

*Christ chose to come to this earth when Rome
occupied Palestine and Judea. The cross was Rome's
answer to all insurrection and rebellion. I'm sure the
cross made a terrible impression on children and adults
in those very difficult times.*

His Fathers Will

*As the cross was carried
it became stained crimson red
coming from the back of our savior as he bled*

*But when Christ stumbled and fell that awful day
Simon was chosen to carry his cross
. . . the rest of the way*

*His strong back took the cross
up to Calvary's hill
Where Christ suffered and died
Oh! It was . . . his fathers will*

22

The Man I Met That Day

I was just a little boy in Jerusalem that day
when an angry crowd appeared
where I would often play

As the crowd came near, a soldier pushed me aside
Then I became so afraid I wanted to run and hide

But then a man
with a crown of thorns upon his head
came carrying a cross
that was stained crimson red

After a few more steps he stumbled to the ground
and as I saw his bloody back
my heart began to pound

As they helped him up to go
I trembled with much fear
and as they took him away
much cursing I could hear

I ran home crying and in mothers arms I lay
Then I told her of Jesus the man I met that day

Oceans of Eternity

A young boy was following his dad along the beach and everywhere his dad went the young boy followed along, stepping in his dad's footprints.

When the dad realized his son was behind him he said, "Son what are you doing?" The son replied, "I'm following you dad."

Whether it's your mate, friends of even a little child we make an impression on their lives. Oh that we would not lead them in the wrong direction.

Dad's Shoes

Dad's shoes! Oh, they didn't fit
But I put them on and walked a bit

Little sister laughed,
then said, "They don't fit"
But it didn't matter, as I walked a bit

Then dad came in and said,
"Take them off son,
there's other ways you can have fun"

So I took them off though I was a little sad
But one day I'll grow up
and be . . . just like my dad

But Jesus called them unto him, and said, suffer little children to come unto me, and forbid them not: for of such is the kingdom of God.   Luke 18:16

Oceans of Eternity

Oh, that our faith would flow like a stream
Oh, that heaven would become part of our dream

We receive life from God,
then we're soon on our way
where we face many decisions
that affects us day by day

Some will decide to follow Jesus
and travel by his light
and be a guide to others
who struggle in the night

But many will travel down a path
that is sinful and wrong
and influence many of their friends
to also come along

Oh! There is a heaven
Oh! There is a hell
As we choose our destiny others follow as well

And just like a stream,
we're approaching oceans of eternity
Either to be with God in his glorious heaven
or suffer forever in hell's great fiery sea

Our Tongue

We truly have the power to curse or to bless, to build up or to tear down, to restore or to destroy, all with our tongue. If we are having a problem with our tongue it's going to take God's help to fix it.

Cursing

Biting our tongue
oh, that would be best
Rather than cursing someone
and causing much distress

For when our speech is harsh
and rages like a storm
It invites heartache and misery
and seldom brings reform

So let's invite God to go with us
wherever we walk
Then ask him to help us
clean up our talk

For when our tongue
gets out of control
We'll need God's cleansing
deep down in our soul

A wholesome tongue is a tree of life
Proverbs 15:4

Our Tongue

Our tongue has the power to curse or to bless
But if we're not careful,
it'll bring about much distress

Oh! We speak words of beauty
Oh! We speak words of grace
But then we speak words that are so out of place

Oh! Someone please tell me
yes, tell me how can this be
that blessings and cursings
both reside inside of me

Now our relationship to the Lord
it can be weak or strong
and this is what determines
how our speech flows along

For if we walk with the Lord each hour of the day
then we'll be on guard about what we have to say

But often it's our loved ones
who often get most of our scorn
Oh! Why don't we begin to talk
like we've been . . . reborn

A Helping Hand

America is the richest nation on the earth. Many people give to the poor and God will bless them for it. Others seem to hoard up their wealth for they have acquired pretty nice nest eggs. Is it possible they're putting more trust in money than God?

Amongst all this wealth the poor are having to struggle along. Every once in a while someone offers a helping hand.

Struggleville

As I looked around, oh what did I see
Many of God's children living in poverty
Mr. Brown's family can't seem to make ends meet
So now the landlord is getting ready
to put them into the street
Then there's Mr. White's family
their car just broke down
So now they can only hope
to hitch a ride into town
And let's not forget Mr. Green
They're threatening to cut off his heat
And if he can't find some work soon,
he may also end up on the street
Oh, and they all live in a town called . . . Struggleville
And they'll all need some help
When it comes time to pay each bill

He that giveth unto the poor shall not lack: but he
that hideth his eyes shall have many a curse.
Proverbs 28:27

A Helping Hand

If we would but look across this great land
We would see many people who need a helping hand
The poor are always with you
Jesus was heard to say
But will we do something about it
as we travel along our way
We often make excuses as we try to fill our nest
But to lay up treasures in heaven,
oh, wouldn't that be best
But somehow we're afraid we won't have enough
So we keep on gathering all our worldly stuff
Jesus told of a widow; two mites she had to give
Her gift was an example of the life she chose to live
The poor we always have with us
Yes, they will always be around
But as they constantly struggle,
will a helping hand be found

Storms of Life

Sometimes we say, "Why me Lord," when a problem comes our way. I had a heart attack, then a few years later I had open heart surgery. These storms of life quickly appeared and I received a stormy blast. Then depression came and it seemed as if I had very little hope

No one is immune to problems. They come to us all and as we get older they seem to come with more severity. Nevertheless if these storms of life pass over we get back on our feet and walk in God's sunlight once again.

Back on My Feet

*The Lord helped me
to get back on my feet
The ground felt good
and oh so sweet*

*As he walks with me now
I have a big grin
The sun has appeared
Oh! It makes me lift up my chin*

The spirit of man will sustain his infirmity; but
A wounded spirit who can bear
Proverbs 18:14

Storms of Life

We all wish for an uncloudy day
Where storms of life are lifted
And gone away

For when they pass over
God's sunlight will then appear
Bringing hope into our soul
and a calming of our fears

Have you ever been healed
are you now okay
Has a problem disappeared
and suddenly gone away

Then walk in God's sunlight
and enjoy the day
and rejoice in the fact
he has sent your storm away

I'm Heaven Bound

One day in the future Christ will return to take
his bride, (the church) to Heaven. Then the great
tribulation on the earth will start
Heaven is going to be a great place and the
bible only gives us glimpses of what it will be like.
Christ is coming with a shout. Let's be ready.
Let's not be ashamed at his appearing. We'll get new
bodies. We'll all be changed.
There'll be no more pain,
no more suffering. What a glorious day that will be!
Just put your trust in the Lord
and you can go with me.

Getting Ready

I'm getting ready
to meet Jesus in the air
I sure hope that I'll also
be able to see you there

On clouds of glory
the saints of God shall meet
Then we'll be with Jesus forever
and our lives will be complete

*16 For the Lord himself shall descend from heaven with
a shout, with the voice of the archangel, and with the
trump of God; and the dead in Christ shall rise first:
17 Then we which are alive and remain shall be caught
up together with them in the clouds, to meet the Lord in
the air, and so shall we ever be with the Lord.*

1Thessalonians 4:16-17

I'm Heaven Bound

*One day soon the Lord,
he will give a shout
Then no Christian will be found
no not one will be about
For we'll all be gone to meet him
Yes, up in the air
Our bodies will be changed
and we won't have a care
Then through those pearly gates
we shall all enter in
We'll be greeting every one
and meeting with our kin
Then on those streets of gold
our Lord he shall walk
We'll feel those nail pierced hands
and with him we shall talk
A glorious day that will be
when the Lord Jesus we shall see
Just put your trust in the Lord
and you can go with me*

Tell Others

What could possibly have been going through the minds of these women when they saw these awesome angels and heard the message that the tomb was empty.
Later Christ told his disciples to go and proclaim the good news of his resurrection to the entire world.

Christ is Risen

Believers!
We must not wait
We must tell others
before it's too late

Christ is risen!
Our words we must proclaim
There's salvation thru him
Oh! Praise his holy name

Repent and be baptized
Yes, from your sins turn
is a message we must deliver
or in hell the lost will burn

And he said unto them. Go ye into all the world,
and preach the gospel to every creature.
Mark 16:15

Tell Others

It was early in the morning,
near the dawning of the day
The savior's tomb was empty
and the guards had fled away

Three days he had lain there,
wrapped from his head to his feet
Now the time had come
and resurrection day was complete

The women as they came
were overcome with fright
For the angels had such beauty
and were such an awesome sight

The tomb is empty,
they heard the angels say
Now go and tell the others
yes, go do it right away

Yes, the tomb is empty,
that's what we must say
We must go tell the world
Yes, we must do it right away

Loosing Our Cool

Some children have been shouted at so long and so often that they probably feel it's the normal thing for parents to do. We shout at a loved one or even a close friend when we become frustrated and angry.

Oh! If we would be wise and break the habit of losing our cool and playing the fool. When we feel the temperature rising we need to call on God's help. What would life be like if God shouted at us every time we disappointed him?

Words of Encouragement

Children are a blessing,
a gift from God above
Sent to earthly parents on wings of pure love
And as our children go through life
they will often stub their toe
Just like we probably did,
not so many years ago
Therefore . . . words of encouragement
is what they will often need
and if they make poor choices
then we should take the lead
We should also remember
God has placed them in our care
So let's begin our day
by lifting them up in prayer

There is that speaketh like the piercing of a sword:
but the tongue of the wise is health. Proverbs 12:18

Losing Our Cool

Every once in a while I raise my voice
and when I do, it's usually a bad choice

We shout at a loved one that we love best
Then it causes everyone to lose their rest

But God is watching as we lose our cool
and so are our neighbors,
as we play the fool

What can we do as we go down life's lane
Shouting and stammering and acting insane

We must try to remain calm
Yes, to the very end
For when we do
then there's a message we send

And then there's also hope
if we would but pray
asking God to keep us calm
at the beginning of each day

Old Mister Anger

It only takes a moment to get angry and then another moment to explode. If we are going to pray when we see anger approaching on the scene, we must do it very quickly.

Yes, we must be ready at a moments notice to ask God for his help in calming us. Prayer, even a very short prayer will help to calm us down in times of anger.

Troubled Children

*May we promptly remember
if anger should come our way
To ask God for his help
in getting through the day*

*For he calms our troubled souls
and helps anger go away
When his troubled children
turn to him and pray*

Be not hasty in thy spirit to be angry; for anger resteth in the bosom of fools.   Ecclesiastes 7:9

Old Mister Anger

Old Mister Anger
You have a friend or two
For heartache and misery often accompany you

And when God's children start down their path
You often travel along to stir up some wrath

But I've got you figured out
for when God's children pray
You just leave them alone and quietly turn away

So every time I see you coming
I say a quick prayer
then when I turn around,
Old Mister Angers not there

If more of God's children would just figure you out
Then they'd begin to pray
and you'd stop your coming about

Why Worry

I know worrying is not good for a person's health. In fact worrying is not good for anything. It turns a smile into a frown and turns our world upside down.

Sooner or later worrying will get the best of us. We must try to deal with it. God can help us not to worry if we will just realize he is in control and that all things will go according to his will. We are his children so let's put our trust and faith in him and his son Jesus Christ.

Old Mister Worry

*When a problem came along,
Old Mister Worry came as well
He was quite annoying
like the constant ringing of a bell*

*And though I bidded him to go
he wanted to stick around
This caused me such discomfort
that my heart began to pound*

*But then I gave the Lord my problem
while kneeling in prayer
Now Old Mister Worry's gone,
for I'm trusting in God's care*

Is any among you afflicted? Let him pray. Is any merry?
let him sing Psalms.   *James 5:13*

Why Worry

Oh! What good does it do to worry
Oh! What good does it do to fear
The Lord will take care of our problems
and without a doubt, he's always near

Oh! Why are we so uneasy
Oh! Why can't we face the day
If we would just look to Jesus
If we would just take time to pray

Oh! Why do we end up doubting
On! Why do we lose our cheer
If we would just count our blessings
then everything would become very clear

So let's not worry o'er the future
Let's not worry what it will bring
Let's put our trust in Jesus the savior
Let's put our trust in Jesus the king

Our Bed

Let's ask Jesus into our hearts and invite him into our lives as we travel down the highway of life. Then he will put joy and peace into our hearts and give us strength to face the day and power to overcome the temptations of sin.

The Miry Clay of Sin

While traveling down a lowly path
we become stuck in the miry clay of sin
and there will never be any hope for us
if we search for power from within

For sin will never give up its grip
lest we get strength from up above
Nor can we be cleansed from its ugly stain
lest we receive what Christ has done with love

For Christ alone can set us free,
yes, he has the power over sin
So let's invite him into our hearts,
then a new life with him will begin

9 That if thou shalt confess with thy mouth the Lord Jesus, and shalt believe in thine heart that God hath raised him from the dead, thou shalt be saved.
10 For with the heart man believeth unto righteousness; and with the mouth confession is made unto salvation.
Romans 10:9-10

Our Bed

We make our bed on this earth below
Then often complain about how things go

But it's never too late to turn things around
If we place our feet on solid ground

Now Jesus is the way
He's the solid rock
Will you trust in him
Can you hear him knock

We've made our bed
We've done things our way
We've turned from God
Now it's time to pray

God forgive my sins
Let me experience your grace
Thank you for sending Jesus
to die in my place

I have shewed you all things, how that so laboring ye ought to support the weak, and to remember the words of the Lord Jesus, how he said, it is more blessed to give than to receive   *Acts 20:35*

Time Keeps Marching On

As we live on this earth we often try to gather as much as we can. But God's word says we are to work extra hare to be able to share with those in need. We save up for vacations and pleasure but those things often invite sin into our lives. Let's ask Jesus to guide and direct our investments. For when we give to the needy, he will pay us back. It's a fountain that never runs dry.

Life's Road

Life's road will bring uncertainty
Life's road will bring us fear
But it also brings us peace and comfort,
just knowing the Lord is near

Each mile we go he will be with us,
for his Spirit abides deep within
He wants to guide and direct us
and help us turn away from sin

Time Keeps Marching On

Time keeps marching on
as we go down life's road
where we meet many travelers,
many who have a heavy load

Many also need a friend
Someone who seems to understand
Many worry o'er the future,
Many need a helping hand

And though God is on his throne
as we go down life's road
He can see the many travelers
He can see their heavy loads

And if we'll just take the time
to help someone along the way
God's looking down from heaven
It's going to be a brighter day

Sunrise

*I believe God gives each of us the ability to praise
and glorify him in prayer. He wants us to start our day
doing just that and if we do, then our lives will be more
meaningful. Then we will be able to get along better
with everyone and will be less likely to yield to the
temptations that come our way.*

Our Songs of Praise

*As the sun rises,
its rays warmly kiss the sky
and as a glorious day begins
we need to pray to God on high
For he's our great creator,
the one who gives us life each day
and he's ready to hear us
as we bow our heads to pray
All praises belong to him
for he even hears the mother robin sing
'Tis her melody of faith,
as she trusts whatever life will bring
Let's likewise trust the Lord of glory
as the sun's rays warmly kiss the sky,
by singing our songs of praise
as we magnify a loving God on high*

From the rising of the sun unto the going down of the
same the Lord's name is to be praised.   Psalm113:3

Sunrise

As the sun rises
Its warmth begins to stir the air
and as a new day begins
let's talk to God in prayer

For its God's amazing grace
that gives us breath each day
Therefore as the sun comes forth,
let's ask him to guide our way

Then the day will have more meaning
We'll listen to the birds as they sing
For after we've talked with God
we'll enjoy more that life will bring

Also we'll get along better with others
for we'll see everything in a different light
For when we talk to God
he encourages us to make all things right

And so as the sun rises
and its warmth begins to stir the air
Let's begin our new day
by talking to God in prayer

.

Sow Seeds With Delight

In many countries to witness for Christ will bring persecution, imprisonment and possibly even death. Jesus told us, "Ye shall be hated of all men for my name's sake." Mark 13:13

Still, we're told to go into all the world and tell others the good news of the gospel of the Lord Jesus Christ. There will be many setbacks but there will also be many rewards. So let's be very brave, even if it means certain persecution and death.

A Crown of Life

Disappointments
Oh! There will be a few
For Satan and his demons
try to destroy all that we do
For they send evil men to threaten
both to kill and to maim
But let's remember to the Lord Jesus
they also did the same

So be of good courage
all ye saints of God
For God will give you power
wherever your feet may trod
Also a crown of life is awaiting
all who will take up their cross
and like our great shepherd Jesus
they will never suffer loss

*32 whosoever therefore shall confess me before men,
him will I confess also before my father which is in
heaven.
33 but whosoever shall deny me before men, him will I
also deny before my father which is in heaven.*

Matthew 10:32-33

Sow Seeds With Delight

*To deny the lord as threats of death come near
or be very brave and show evil men no fear*

*Alas . . . . to deny the Lord Jesus
would bring us much shame
for we have told others to believe on his name*

*And surely the Lord above
will keep guard of our mind
To keep us from denying him
in front of them who are blind*

*Therefore let's take hold of the plow
and let our furrows be straight
Let's tell others of Jesus
before it becomes too late*

*As the new ground is broken
we'll sow seeds with delight
There'll be a bountiful harvest
and we'll sleep contented at night*

'Twas A Dream

Did I really dream this dream? Well I did dream some of it and that's why I wrote the poem.

I hope someday I'll get escorted into heaven and get to meet my savior the Lord Jesus Christ.

I hope you enjoy my poem for it was fun to write.

Someday Soon

Someday soon
Oh! It could happen any day
My soul will leave this body,
on planet earth to decay

But, my soul will travel upwards
Yes, to heaven up above
Where I'll meet with Jesus
my savior whom I love

And the twelve gates were twelve pearls; every several gate was one pearl: and the street of the city was of pure gold as it were transparent glass.
Revelation 21:21

'Twas A Dream

I dreamed my heart failed one day
Then my soul began to float away
Although I could see my body down below
I felt that it would soon be time to go
As I looked around, evil spirits I could see
but then two angels came and took hold of me
We entered a tunnel as dark as could be
and as we traveled on a light I could see
They took me on to heavens door
where I would live forevermore
Friends and family were waiting for me
and as I went around, I was happy as I could be
I felt that soon, Jesus I would behold
as I walked along those streets of gold
But that wasn't immediately going to be
for I woke up . . . . 'twas a dream you see

A Special Friend

Are you willing to be someone's special friend?
We all need one. We sometimes neglect to, "be there," when someone needs us the most.
Going through divorce, the loss of a child or parent, sickness, or even depression are just a few of the life storms that buffet us with all their might.
When I had my heart attack, I had many friends to encourage me as I was healing both physically and emotionally.

Be There

When we hear a friends having troubles,
we may lift them up in prayer
But we also need to take some time
just too . . . . be there

For in times of sickness
and in times of despair
They'll need that special someone
who will . . . . be there

That very special friend,
the one who tells them that they care
They're hoping we will be by their side
they're hoping we will . . . . be there

I will never leave thee, nor forsake thee
Hebrews 13:5

A Special Friend

There will be times
when we need to hold on tight
As life's storms begin to buffet us
with all of their might

Cancer, heart attacks, depression
Oh! They're just a few
of the storms of life
descending on me and you

And although God's word is helpful
during these times of fear and stormy wind
It will also be a time
when we need God to send a special friend

Someone who understands,
someone who knows our fright
Someone who'll be close by
and go with us through the long night

Thank God for his word and promises,
but may he send that special friend
Someone to help us hold on tight
through these storms that life will send

And the peace of God, which
passeth all understanding,
shall keep your hearts and minds
through Christ Jesus.
Philippians 4:7

Drink From His Fountain

When we receive forgiveness of our sins it brings
great peace to our hearts and minds. This peace that
passeth understanding should
remain in our hearts and
minds as we face difficulties and
pressures of life daily.
Sometimes we need to remind ourselves just who
we are in Jesus Christ. We're God's children who will
one day be with him eternally in glory.

Worries And Fears

Worries and fears
Oh, how they weigh me down
Then my soul begins to doubt
and my heart begins to pound
But if I bring to remembrance,
God's goodness and his grace
Then all my worries and fears go away
and peace comes in to take their place
So I try to keep my mind on God
and talk to him throughout the day
Then leave my worries and fears far behind
as I travel along my way

Drink From His Fountain

I awoke one morning
and was as uneasy as I could be
until I thought of Jesus who began to set me free

Yes, he began to bring a calm
at the beginning of my day
He brought it into my soul when I began to pray

So if you feel anxious and troubles are on the way
Just turn them over to Jesus and he will be your stay

He has the power to turn our darkness into light
To calm all our fears and take away our fright

For when our storm is raging
the Lord Jesus will draw near
In the midst of all our problems
he can calm all our fears

And if we drink from his fountain
the water of life will flow
Bringing to us a calm,
while down the road of life we go

Walking With the Lord

We live in a world where we will often experience difficulties and hardships. As we walk with the Lord we often wonder why he doesn't make life just a little easier.

Life's Great Trials

*Our love for this world
how it becomes ever so small
As life's great trials
seem to bring our hope and faith to a stall
For when we go through these trials
though God's grace is always there
We can't always see past
the hardships and difficulties we bear
But if we will just remember,
things of this world are passing away
and God is preparing his children
to live up in heaven one day
Yes, far better things are waiting
and it's no shame if we should die
For as we turn to face eternity,
God will be there to hear our cry
And when we get to heaven,
we'll not want to come back
To face more of life's great trials
and trade a mansion for a shack*

*For our light affliction which is but for a moment,
worketh for us a far more exceeding and eternal weight
of glory; 2 Corinthians 4:17*

Walking With the Lord

*When we walk with the Lord,
everything won't always go our way
Storms will sometimes show up
to shatter the calm of our day*

*Have you lost a loved one
Is someone in poor health
Maybe there's depression,
or maybe you've lost your wealth*

*Life's road will bring heartaches
Troubles . . . . there'll be more than a few
But remember through them all
the Lord is walking with you*

*And after these storms pass over
the sun will display its rays
Also heaven will be waiting
when we come to the end of our days*

The Earth

In the beginning God created the heavens and the earth. He placed Adam and Eve in the garden of Eden to keep and dress it. What a beautiful place that must have been.

God wants us to get along with each other and take care of the earth and not pollute it. Sadly we are not getting along and we don't take care of the earth.

Good News

As I searched for how all life began
I then turned to the bible
and found God's good news for man

From Genesis to Revelation,
a holy God remained the same
It was a story of redemption
and this is why Jesus came

He's the Alpha and Omega
Yes, the beginning and the end
By him all things were made
and by him comes forgiveness of sin

My help cometh from the Lord, which made heaven and earth   *Psalm 121:2*

The Earth

When God created the earth,
he placed it way out in space
'Twas a lovely home for Adam and his race

He gave them a sun by day and a moon by night
With millions of stars each giving off their light

With seasons that come and seasons that go
'Twas sunshine, or rain, or sleet, or snow

Yes, God made the earth
and he saw it was good
Therefore let us rejoice
and treat his creation as we should

We might plant a tree that grows very high
and invites birds of the air to rest by and by

Then as we wake up daily to God we can pray
and thank earth's creator
as it spins along its way

*But my God shall supply all your needs according to
his riches in glory by Christ Jesus. Philippians 4:19*

God's Hands

*As a Christian all our problems belong to God, for
we are his children. Just like it's our responsibility to
take care of our children, it's his responsibility to take
care of us and he has promised to do so.
God allows some problems to come into our lives to
help us grow. We must trust that
he will be there for us,
even in our darkest hours.*

Problems

*Problems
Oh! I've had some it's true
And as they came along
I often got sad and blue*

*But through them all
I knew God was there
For I met him every day
when we fellowshipped in prayer*

God's Hands

I looked over my problems
and placed them in God's hands
But then I began to doubt and try to take command
But God in his wisdom let me take control
But then my heart became heavy
as my life began to unfold
For my problems were great
and brought anguish to my mind
Each time I tried to work them out,
no path could I find
Then my relations with others
became strained day by day
When tempers began to flair
then I began to pray
I told the Lord I couldn't do it
and that he must take control
That I'd made such a mess
it was tearing at my soul
Now I still have a lot of problems,
but I've placed them back in God's hands
but hope has returned
since I'm no longer in command

He shall not be afraid of evil tidings: his heart is fixed,
Trusting in the Lord   *Psalms 112:7*

Worrying

God's children will never be worry free because there are so many things that trouble us. Any life threatening event is sure cause for worry.

But if we will begin to realize that God is in control and that nothing happens without his permission then we should begin to be comforted. Peace will come to those who trust in God with all their hearts.

Tested

Old Mister Worry, knocked on my door
and after I let him in, I began to pace the floor
Then all my inner peace left me right away
and as my faith became tested,
I thought it best to pray
So I asked the Lord if he would take control
and allow my inner peace to come back into my soul
As my faith became strengthened,
great peace came deep inside
Because realizing God was in control,
made Old Mister Worry run and hide

Worrying

I got up today
but I was hesitant to pray
Worries had came along
and gotten in my way

So I put God off for a little while
But he soon reminded me
that I was his child

So I said a quick prayer to him right away
But I still felt uncomfortable
the rest of the day

When I asked him later why I still felt bad
Then he told me I hadn't trusted him
with all that I had

I hadn't left my worries in his tender loving care
And my trust in him,
well, it just wasn't there

Oh! That we might begin
to trust in God more and more
Then we might see most of our worrying
go out through the door

*And the Lord God planted a garden
eastward in Eden; and there he put the
man whom he had formed. Genesis 2:8*

A Day at the Park

*This poem, "A day at the park," makes you
think of a beautiful garden like God planted for Adam
and Eve.
I think God wants us to take time off from our
busy schedules to be with our families and his marvelous creation.*

Walking in the Shade

*As we frolicked at the park and soaked in the sun
I felt God was watching
while we were having fun*

*Oh! He must have been there
walking in the shade
Looking at the things his hands had made*

*He saw the flowers with colors so bright
He saw each bird while they were in flight*

*He sent the breeze that cooled us that day
and as we sat down to eat
he watched us bow and pray*

A Day in The Park

There was a nice park at the end of a lane
We went there one day
though we thought it might rain

The children began playing
and were as happy as could be
As they rolled on the grass
it looked so good to me

The birds were singing a pleasant song
The squirrels were fidgety
as they scampered along

The ducks were paddling along
with their big webbed feet
and began quacking loudly
as we threw them bread to eat

The skies began to clear
and gave everyone much delight
Then we knew right away
everything would be all right

I sat down on a bench just to soak in some sun
Now a day at the park sure turned out to be fun

*And he arose, and rebuked the wind, and said unto the
sea, peace, be still, and the wind ceased, and there
was a great peace.*   *Mark 4:39*

A Peaceful Calm

*What a Lord we have! He's able to calm the sea
and stop the wind, and he's able to cause the turmoil
inside us to subside.
When I wrote this poem I had gone through
several days of inner turmoil and was anxious about
many things. So this poem is a prayer to the Lord.
God wants us to allow him to take control of
our life. If he's in control I feel more secure, but when
I try to take control there's no peace inside.*

Inner Peace

*Lord if you will
just take control
There will be inner peace
within my soul*

*Bid the winds to stop
then calm the raging sea
Then all the turmoil will subside
that's stirring inside of me*

A Peaceful Calm

Lord give us a peaceful day
Let the inner turmoil be turned away

Let us not be anxious but may we always pray
Asking for your help at the beginning of each day

Forever guiding,
may you lead the way
Directing each step as we move through the day

Give us courage to stand up for what is right
Knowing that we are children of the light

May we trust that you are ever so near
For just feeling your presence
will help calm all our fears

May we place all our hope in you to save
Knowing it was for us that your life you gave

Yes, may a peaceful calm fill us right away
Lord, just speak the word
yes, do it for us we pray

But Jesus called them unto him and said, suffer little
children to come unto me, and forbid them not for
such is the kingdom of God Luke 18:16

Little Shoes and Little Feet

I wrote this poem when my granddaughter brought
her shoe to me to untie a knot in her shoelace.
As I untied the knot I thought about how precious
a little child is and I wondered how many miles those
little feet would carry her. I also wondered what paths
she would travel.
I take my granddaughters to church, but I need to
do so much more. I hope God will give me more wisdom
to help them in their walk through life.

The Knot

I untied the knot in her little shoe
Then prayed for her
like most granddaddies do
As I looked at those precious little feet
I prayed to God
that her life might be more complete
When I placed those little shoes
on her little feet
I gave her a gentle hug
for granddaughters are oh, so sweet

Little Shoes and Little Feet

Thank God for little shoes and little feet
A blessing from above so beautiful and so sweet
A child is precious in every way
each step that they take
Should brighten our day
As they walk through life
they need our guidance each day
and when they stumble and fall
encouragement is needed right away
Little feet that run,
oh, may they be swift and sure
Accompanied by a heart
that is sweet and pure
Little feet that go pitter patter,
early into the night
Little feet that we cleanse
and tuck in bed out of sight
Many prayers will be needed
for the steps our children make
For God in his mercy
gives each a path to take
As we place little shoes
on our children's little feet
Giving a gentle hug
will make our lives more complete

Study to shew thyself approved unto God, a workman that needeth not to be ashamed, rightly dividing the word of truth.   *2 Timothy 2:15*

Be Of Good Courage

Whenever God has an important job to do, he often has chosen a few faithful men and women to do the job. Abraham, Joseph, Moses, Peter, Paul and Mary are just a few examples.

God still has many important jobs for us to do. In fact all his jobs are important and we need to be ready and willing to be used of him when the time comes. He will give us the strength and power to fulfill any task he has for us to do. So let's be ready.

Study and Pray

God has many tasks for his children to do
He may call on me or he may call on you
But whoever he calls he'll give them power
to resist and overcome Satan
in their most critical hour
But we must be willing
to study God's word and pray
Lest we be found ignorant
and God chooses another way

Be of Good Courage

When God has an important job to do
He will sometimes send only one or two

We think that more is always best
But sometimes God uses a few
to excite all the rest

He often uses the weak to confound the strong
But it's always his power that helps them along

So if you want God to use you in a mighty way
Then you must take time to often study and pray

For you may be the only light
someone will ever see
But, you must be ready
And preparation is the key

Then when God reveals what he has for you to do
Be of good courage,
he's getting ready to use you

One Hand on The Key board

*Our small church needed a pianist, so one of our
newest members offered to fill in. She often played at
home, but only with one hand because a stroke had
left her unable to use the other hand.
But Mrs. Jean Sierra did such a good job she
became our full time pianist. She was a wonderful testi-
mony to everyone that we should never give up and
always do our best to serve God.*

Carry On

*If the Lord allows an infirmity to come our way
He'll often give us strength to carry on each day*

*Cancer, diabetes, heart attack
or even a stroke
are just a few illnesses that beset God's folk*

*And through their heartaches they look for a way
to praise the Lord and carry on each day*

*One plays a melody
and it ascends to God's throne
Oh! They may be weakened
but God never leaves them alone*

The spirit of a man will sustain his infirmity; but a wounded spirit who can bear?   *Proverbs 18:14*

With One Hand on the Keyboard

With one hand on the keyboard,
the piano she did play
Lifting our spirit with music
And melody for the day
She gave us such encouragement,
whenever she played her part
For during our church services,
her music stimulated our hearts
With one hand on the keyboard,
the notes began to ring
Then we lifted our voices to Jesus
our Lord, our savior, our king
Because she never gave up,
It was an inspiration to us all,
To always do our very best,
to answer the Lord's call
With one hand on the keyboard,
the other was at her side
Silenced by a terrible stroke,
however God helped her to abide
But, one day up in heaven
those piano notes again will ring,
As we lift our voices to Jesus,
our Lord, our savior, our king

Thoughts of Despair

I wrote these poems when I was in deep depression and this is exactly how I felt.

I wasn't sure if I should include these poems in my book for I am actually ashamed that I was so down and out, but maybe someone will read it and and say, "That's what I'm going through."

I've came a long way since then and it's like I've came out of a long dark tunnel into the sunlight.

There's hope if you're going through depression. I know exactly how you feel. The main thing is to never give up.

Depression in My Cup

As I sat there alone,
There was depression in my cup
And though each sip caused me pain,
I was not ready to give up

For God will never give me
more than I can bear
Miracles will surely happen,
For I'm under his tender loving care

The troubles of my heart are enlarged; o bring me out of my distresses.   *Psalm 25:17*

Thoughts of Despair

Thoughts of despair, they won't go away
They keep coming back
at the beginning of each day
They turn my smile into a frown
and the weight on my back
it just keeps me down
And while this feeling of no hope
brings torture to me
My loved ones are affected
and want to see me set free
So they give me encouragement
and wish me well
But the thoughts still remain
and despair rings like a bell
I'm told by others
that they have sometimes felt this way
yes, these thoughts have come
and saddened their day
But no one should have to go
through this kind of despair
May the Lord deliver me
and place me under his tender loving care

A friend loveth at all times.   Proverbs 17:17

A Little Balcony

We like to keep moving on in life, but sometimes we have to take a rest. It sometimes causes us to reflect back on our life. Where we've been, what we've done. Sometimes we wish we could go back and change things but that's not possible.

Many things will cause you to retreat to life's little balcony where you try to get a glimpse of the road ahead and examine the road you have just traveled. Cancer, heart disease, diabetes, depression and mental illnesses are just a few.

It's so important for friends to come and encourage you to get back on the road of life and accompany you along the way.

They Care

When they heard of my illness,
oh, they came right away
offering words of encouragement
that helped me make it through the day

As I got back on my feet,
they were still there
Then they helped me along
and told me they care

A Little Balcony

As I traveled down life's road
I needed to take a rest
So I retired to a little balcony
where my view would be best
Life's road had many travelers,
some were hurrying along their way
Destiny seemed to have them by the hand
to guide them day by day
But when I glanced back down the road
from whence I'd came
It had a feeling of regret
and mistakes were to blame
I wished I could go back
and make all things right
But I must travel on ahead
and not be filled with fright
For the road leading to the past
weary travelers can not take
They must continue on ahead
though the road has brought heartache
I looked and heard friends calling
from the road down below
They invited me to come along
and said, "It's time to go"
So I left the little balcony
and down life's road we went
Then I said a special prayer
to thank God for the friends he'd sent

The wages of sin is death but the gift of God is eternal life through Jesus Christ our Lord.   Romans 6:23

Temptations

Ever since Adam and Eve were tempted in the Garden of Eden, Satan has been tempting us to sin and he is very good at it. We all have our weaknesses but he will leave us alone if we will just resist the temptations.

When we fall into sin God is always there encouraging us to repent and turn away from our sins and come back to him.

Seek Heavenly Things

Temptations to sin
Seems like we all get our share
And when they come along,
God watches us . . . . with care

Sometimes we yield,
seeking the pleasure sin often brings
When we should quickly turn away
and instead seek heavenly things

But as the pleasure of sin begins to wane,
God will always prick each heart
to come back to him
and from our sins ever depart

*13 Let no man say when he is tempted, I am tempted of
God; for God cannot be tempted with evil, neither
tempteth he any man;*
*14 But every man is tempted, when he is drawn away
of his own lust, and enticed.*
*15 then when lust hath conceived, it bringeth forth sin;
and sin, when it is finished, bringeth forth death.*
James 1:13-15

Temptations

*Oh! Why don't we just do the right thing
for when temptations come along
we often yield to what they bring
Then uneasy days our sins bring no doubt
as our fellowship with God is cast all about
Also our inner peace will leave
and go its own way
While our relations with others
often becomes strained day by day
Therefore victory won't come unless we repent
So let's agree with God
and remember why Christ was sent
Then we'll be restored
and have fellowship with God once more
Instead of yielding to temptations
and walking through their open door*

He's Calling

*Running from God will cause all kinds of misery.
We will never be satisfied until we snuggle close to the
Lord. Oh! That we would desire to be close to him.*

*Jesus is calling, is tenderly calling,
calling all sinners . . . . come home*

Under His Wings

*I strayed away from God
Yes, I wanted to be on my own
I felt I knew what was best
Yes, I wanted to be left alone*

*So I became disobedient
and went the way of sin
As my path became darker,
there came great fear within*

*But I heard the Lord calling
'Twas the sound of pure love
Now I've come back under his wings
Now he whispers to me from above*

Yea, they turned back and tempted God, and limited the
holy one of Israel.   *Psalm 78:41*

He's Calling

From God, we sometimes run away
when our doubts and fears
cause us to disobey

And our path always heads downhill
as we run away from God
and his perfect will

Nevertheless very compassionately,
God loves us still
And he's faithfully calling to us
from the top of the hill

Therefore, let's repent
and once again seek his perfect will
Then he'll give us strength
to climb back up the hill

Evening and morning, and at noon, will I pray and cry aloud; and he shall hear my voice.   Psalm 55:17

Call On Him

We can call on God in prayer, morning, noon and night and he has promised in the bible to hear us. It is an honor and privilege to talk to god in prayer.

Take The Time To Pray

Whatever the situation,
whatever the time of day
God will be listening,
when we . . . . take the time to pray

It may be in the morning,
or when the sun goes down
It may be when we stop to rest,
or on our way to town

Each moment will be an opportunity
to fellowship with God each day
But it will only happen
when we . . . . take the time to pray

Call On Him

Oh! That we would often take care
to call on God, with a sweet prayer

For he listens
Yes, from heaven up above,
To all who are seeking
his fellowship and love

He's able to heal and ready to touch
He's able to provide and give us so much

And he's not as far away as some might think
Just a moment in time,
much quicker than a blink

And he's not angry as some might say
But willing to hear
if we will just take time to pray

Therefore let's draw near to God
by the blood of Jesus his son,
into a wonderful relationship
as our work on earth is done

Sweet Dreams

It's not good to leave God out of our day, but sometimes it happens when we get busy and don't take time with him in fellowship and prayer.

When we leave God out, then other things take God's place such as anxiety and doubt. Our getting along with others becomes more difficult and there is less inner peace.

God is always close by and all we have to do is call on him in prayer. When we do our day will go better and our nights will bring about sweet dreams.

A Day without God

As I left God out of my busy day
All of our sweet fellowship just went away

It was replaced with anxiety and doubt
My relations with others were strained,
as I hurried about

To ask for Gods help
Oh! I just couldn't take the time
For I busy working and making my dime

And it left me very sad,
when my days work was done
For a day without God
took away all the fun

17. Pray without ceasing.
18. In everything give thanks: for this is the will of
God in Christ Jesus concerning you.
1 Thessalonians 5:17-18

Sweet Dreams

It was getting time to go to bed
But, I had an urge to pray instead

I hadn't invited God into my busy day
so I felt guilty, as I began to pray

When I apologized to him
He said, "That's okay
a lot of folks do me that way

They choose to walk alone
Then begin to wonder where I've gone

But I'm always ever so near
and if they pray, I'll always hear"

When I asked him for . . . . a good night
He then said,
"Sweet dreams, I'll wake you at dawn's early light"

Faith and Courage

There will always be pain and suffering in this world. Mothers suffer greatly during childbirth and when we die often there's great suffering.

One day we will step through a door that leads to a life with God in heaven. There'll be no more death, neither pain, nor suffering. But until then, let's have faith and courage to face what life has is store, knowing that God will be with us to help in our time of need.

Suffering

*Sometimes we're called to suffer
and it seems more than we can bear
We often think . . . . why me Lord
and may wonder . . . . does he care
But Jesus also suffered,
he was the perfect and sinless man
Choosing to die on a cruel cross
he revealed to us God's holy plan
He took our place completely,
It was the just for the unjust
Our sins are now placed on him,
when on him we place our trust
So Jesus knows about suffering,
he knows and sees our pain
As we place our faith in him,
we have redemption from sin to gain*

17. The troubles of my heart are enlarged: o bring thou me out of my distresses.
18. Look upon mine affliction and my pain; and forgive my sins.   Psalm 25:17-18

Faith and Courage

We'll have trials and tribulations
in this world down below
And we'll often get discouraged,
no matter where we go
Therefore let's have faith and courage
as troubles comes our way
For God wants us to be brave
as we live in this world each day
So when we experience pains and heartaches,
let's seek Gods help and care
Then demonstrate faith and courage
after we've talked to him in prayer
He is the Lord of glory
we can trust him day by day
So let's begin to show our faith and courage
and chase our doubts and fears away
Let's also remember . . . .
God knows how much we can bear
So let's place all the rest
in his tender loving care

Casting all your care upon him for he careth for you.
1 Peter 5:7

Carefree

As I write these poems, it seems that God is telling me to practice what I preach. We all need to realize that we are in God's hands and all things will go according to his will and plan.

Let's tell God that we're going to place all our faith and trust in him. Then as God sees our faith and trust, we can expect miracles to happen.

If We Trusted God

If we trusted God,
much like a little child
Then some of our problems
would often turn out to be mild

If we trusted God,
with a strong and steadfast heart,
Then hope and faith would return
while many worries would depart

If we trusted God,
and would take time to pray
Then peace would come in like a flood,
as fear and stress flew away

A merry heart maketh a cheerful countenance:
but by sorrow of the heart the spirit is broken.

Proverbs 15:13

Carefree

Oh! The sweet laughter that we often hear
coming from children we love so dear
So why shouldn't we like children be
So full of life and so carefree
Maybe it's our worries that keep us down
They turn our laughter into a frown
Can worry change things one little whit
Can worry change the outcome one little bit
God is with us each step of the way
as we travel our path from day to day
So let's trust him as we fellowship in prayer
Then give him our burdens to share
Then he'll give us merry hearts
We'll see dark clouds lift
as fear and worry departs

Small Stepping Stones

We will have trouble and difficulties as we go down our paths, but God has promised to go with us and deliver us from them. Amen.

God's Unseen Hand

When difficulties come,
we often stumble on our path
But God will be there
As we begin to face life's wrath

And if our faith remains strong,
we will begin to feel God's unseen hand,
that begins to lift us up
and helps us to understand

Then once back on our feet,
we'll soon get back on our way
And as life goes on
God will be there to help us each day

The righteous cry, and the Lord heareth, and deliver-
eth them out of all their troubles.   *Psalm 34:17*

Small Stepping Stones

While walking down life's pathway
difficulties are often just up ahead
But if we ask God to go with us
there'll be nothing to dread
Therefore let's walk with courage
and not be filled with fear
Then we'll experience great peace
just knowing the Lord is near
For he holds our future
in the palms of his hands
and with him by our side
we can meet all that life demands
For the difficulties we will face
Are merely small stepping stones
That brings us closer to God
and his glorious throne
Also each stepping stone will offer us
his fellowship and love
Till it's time to lay down our heads
and wake up in heaven up above

The Lord is my shepherd; I shall not want. Psalm 23:1

Gentle Shepherd

What a Lord we have, he is the shepherd who is able to meet all our needs in this life and the life to come. We need to follow him and not stray away from his voice.

If you belong to him and you stray, he is willing to leave the ninety and nine and come find you and bring you home. Why? Because you belong to him. When he starts out with one hundred sheep, he will not lose any because he is the good shepherd.

Blessings Untold

He strayed away from the Lord and his little flock
To many of the faithful it must have been a shock

But, after God's word revealed his sin
He began to see the dark places he had been

As he repented long into the night
He then saw the Lord coming
with his bright light

Now he's brought him back into the sheepfold
And now he's receiving many blessings untold

Gentle Shepherd

Gentle shepherd
Lead me into paths that I should take
Guide my way in the decisions I must make

May I follow you
and allow you to take control
while I'm on my journey
and my life begins to unfold

Protect me from danger
that might loom up ahead
Lead me into greener pastures,
where my soul will be fed

May I not be deceived and wonder away
Oh! From your gentle voice
may I never, never stray

Gentle Jesus,
my shepherd throughout the day
Anoint me with thy precious oil
and cleanse all my sins away

31 Let all bitterness, and wrath, and anger, and clamor and evil speaking, be put away from you, with all malice; 32 and be ye kind one to another, tenderhearted, forgiving one another, even as God for Christ's sake hath forgiven you.   *Ephesians 4:31-32*

Look Ahead

*There are many things that weigh us down, hold us
back, keep us from moving on
ahead in life. Fear, worry
anger, bitterness, and unforgiveness are just a few
things that tend to hold us back.
We need to make up our minds where we want to
live. Will we live in the past of present? We can look
ahead. We can forgive and forget.
So let's begin to walk
daily in a path of love, forgiveness, and kindness.*

Set Free

*My mind has been quite busy,
bringing back old hurts and pains
But when I begin to think of Jesus
his love for me is all that remains
So each time my past overwhelms me,
bringing old hurts and pains deep within
I begin to think of Jesus
and how he forgave me of all my sins
Then I try to use Christ's example
of the great mercy he showered on me
And give others the gift of forgiveness
for my troubled soul wants to be . . . . set free*

Look Ahead

Let's look ahead
and not be known for looking back
Forever moving forward,
not known for being slack

Yesterday is gone and today is a new day
May we not live in the past,
but strive to live a new way

For the past can be an anchor
and we need to be set free
So let's draw it up
then good sailing there will be

An anchor of bitterness,
an anchor of strife,
An anchor of unforgiveness
can hold us back in life

We can let old wounds heal
we can sing a new song
We can forgive others,
then begin to sail on along

Children of God

What an honor to be called children of God and its all because of what Christ has done for us on Calvary.

When we think of children, we generally think of young people, but we're all children no mater the age if we belong to God. One day in heaven we will be eternally young and never grow old. Hallelujah!

Never Grow Old

This body of mine,
well it's growing old
But when I pass away
a new life will unfold

There'll be no more suffering,
there'll be no more pain
I'll go to be with Jesus
yes, I'll have heaven to gain

And it's a place where you
. . . . never grow old
And you can walk with Jesus
Yes, on streets of pure gold

For ye are the children of God by faith in Christ Jesus
Galatians 3:26

Children of God

As we toil and struggle while traveling earth's sod
Oh! What an honor to be called children of God

Adopted into his family by his amazing grace
We await the day we will see him face to face

But until then an ambassador we can be
Telling others of Christ and how he sets men free

For the name of Jesus,
some have never heard
But they can soon know him
when we give out God's word

So let's go forward as Christians by name
Telling of the Lord Jesus without any shame

Then a new life will belong
to all who will believe
In God's only son and him will receive

A Dream

Sometimes the pressures of life just make us want to run away and hide. We can't always change our circumstances but we can begin to look at them differently.

God wants us to share our pressures, heartaches, and problems with him. When we do we will begin to feel God's great peace.

One day we will be able to leave all the cares of this world behind and experience what God has prepared for us in heaven.

Wonderful Love

Pressures and problems
Oh! How they weigh me down
Then I loose my smile and out comes a frown

But if I fellowship with Jesus,
problems of the world go away
For my spirit soars to heaven,
when I take the time to pray

So I take my daily trips,
yes, to heavenly portals up above
Where I talk alone with Jesus,
and bask in his wonderful love

And God shall wipe away all tears from their eyes;
and there shall be no more death, neither sorrow,
nor crying, neither shall there be any more pain
for the former things are passed away.
Revelation 21:4

A Dream

We all want to have a happy day
Where pressures of life have gone away

Where there's no anxiety within
And a peaceful calm has become our best friend

A day when we all can get along
And everyone is singing a pleasant song

Where neither sickness, nor pain can be found
Neither heartache, nor worry to keep us down

Maybe, it's just a dream I see,
Or maybe up in heaven I'd be

And I saw the dead, small and great, stand before God; and the books were opened: and another book was opened, which is the book of life: and the dead were judged out of those things which were written in the books according to their works.
Revelation 20:12

Our Life Story

We're all writing a story book about ourselves and it's called, "Our Life Story." Each day we write new information in our book. Some of it is good and some of it is bad.
One day when our life is over we will get to take our book with us to meet God. Some of our book we will be proud of but some we will be ashamed of. But it's all there written by our own hand.

Favor With God

If we refuse to consider our sin
Then there'll be no victory for us to win

But if we repent and change our ways
We'll have favor with God and see better days

Then when life's books are opened,
eternal life will be there
For Christ will have washed our sins
in his blood with care

Our Life Story

Our life is like a story
and everyone has a story to tell
We each are writing our life story
and with God's help it will turn out well
Each story will have its beginning
and it will also have its end
But how we live our lives each day,
will determine the message we send
And because each life is so unique
and no two people are the same
We will each write a different story
and it will have nothing to do with our name
Everyday we will write a new chapter,
a chapter in a great book
Sometimes our chapter will be secret,
sometimes we will let others take a look
But God knows what we're writing,
he knows what's in our book
and one day we'll go to face him,
where all heaven will take a look
So let's continue on with our writing,
let's take a firm grip of our pen,
let's show great love to others
and let God take care of us till the end

We'll Meet Again

I wrote these poems after talking to friends
who had lost a mate after many years of marriage.
the bible describes a husband and a wife as one
flesh and when we lose a mate, it is like losing a
part of our own body. May God give comfort to all
who have lost their mates.

Walking Alone

God gives us a mate,
we then walk hand in hand
and as the years roll by,
we leave footprints in the sand

Then one day it happens,
our mate leaves our side
for God calls them home
and so alone we must abide

And as we walk alone,
with one set of footprints in the sand
We reminisce o'er the days
when we both walked hand in hand

And although we are saddened,
for one half of us is gone
We receive strength to continue,
for God promises to never leave us alone

Many waters cannot quench love, neither can the floods drown it: if a man would give all the substance of his house for love, it would utterly be contemned.

Song of Solomon 8:7

We'll Meet Again

I'm on a journey,
but one day it will end
And when I first met my wife
she was more than my best friend

We both traveled along
Yes, we both walked hand in hand
The journey brought us many rewards,
life seemed to have few demands

But as we grew older
and gray hairs came my way
Sickness also came along
and so my lovely wife went away

Since she went away,
I must finish my course alone
But one day I'll meet her again,
for she's waiting near God's throne

O death, where is thy sting? O grave where is thy victory?   *1 Corinthians 15:55*

Traveling On

*Heaven is going to be a wonderful place, yet we
have a certain reluctance when
it comes to facing death.
God will give us peace as we face this mysterious
door that leads to eternity. God's
word has much to say
about heaven and hell and both places are real.
If we have faith then we can have assurance of
eternal life with God, Jesus and the holy angels. Ask
Jesus to save you and give you eternal life with him.*

The Other Side

*If we could get a peek of
The other side
Maybe we wouldn't be afraid
if we suffered and died*

*If we could see those streets of pure gold
and if Jesus we could simply behold*

*Then peace would flow like a stream
and heaven would become part of our dream*

Traveling On

We're heading for that day
when it'll be our time to go away

Death . . .We don't like to think about it
And we would probably like
to put it off a bit

And we certainly don't want to suffer pain
Even though we may have heaven to gain

But life as we know it is surely going to end
Yes, we'll go out like a flame
blown by the wind

But heaven will be waiting
to all who will pray
Asking God for forgiveness
as light is sent their way

I guess I could tell you not to have fear
But most folks have some
as the end draws near

Our Last Sunsets

As my body gets older I have had to face many health problems along the way. It causes me to think about what the future holds for me. I see old age or as some might say, "Golden years," just up ahead.

Our natural instinct is to wish time would slow down. We just don't want to grow old for it brings more poor health as our bodies just seem to wear out. But time won't slow down and worrying doesn't help. We must have faith that God will help us go through the last leg of life's journey.

My Rocking Chair

The wind is often present,
Sometimes blowing against my face
But I feel the Lord's presence
as I approach the finish of my race
And since heaven is my hope
therefore I will not despair,
As I get ready to leave this world
and my rocking chair
And when I get there,
Yes, on the other side,
Let there be no sadness
When you hear that I've died
Yes, the sun is sinking lower,
So don't forget to lift me up in prayer
For I'll soon be leaving this world
and my rocking chair

For by me thy days shall be multiplied, and the years
of thy life shall be increased.   *Proverbs 9:11*

Our Last Sunsets

As we travel down life's path,
old age is waiting up ahead
Tomorrow we will be there
but let there be no dread

For we can trust in tomorrow
yes, we can welcome the day
If we ask Jesus to go with us
and let him lead the way

Then when old age comes to meet us
as we travel down our path,
We'll be able to face one of life's last enemies
As old age demonstrates its wrath

For Jesus knows our future
and he knows our destiny
Heaven will be waiting
as he leads us into eternity

So while we experience our last sunsets,
let's not face them all alone
Let's ask Jesus to go with us
then take us to heaven and God's holy throne

When I started this book I was sixty years old. If we have the ability then we should keep working. God always has something for his children to do. Even those past sixty.

It's Not Best

Will we retire from God's work
and take a long rest
When deep down in our heart
we know it's not best

And while it may be true,
that we have fought a good fight
Will we now sit idly by,
with more victories in sight

God has much more that needs to be done
And there are many more victories
that needs to be won

One day life's battles will be o'er
Then we can rest with God
and be with him forevermore

But until then let's get back into the fight
For the earth is still ready
to receive more of God's light

Poems
For
Special Days

Thanksgiving Day

Turkey and dressing and gravy too
Oh, why do I feel God is watching
Over me and you

Yes, I feel God is watching from up above
Showering this nation with his pure love

For we have liberties and freedoms,
Combined with education and wealth
We also have doctors and nurses
To take care of our health

We're called the home of the brave
And the land of the free
Yes, we're a blessed nation
From sea to shining sea

Therefore as we gather around the table
On this Thanksgiving Day
Let's be a thankful people
As we take the time to pray

Yes! Turkey and dressing and gravy too
Oh! Thank you Lord
For being faithful and true

Autumn Colors

The leaves are changing colors
Oh! What a beautiful sight
Some rustle under my feet
As I watch others fall in flight

Yes, autumn seems to be whispering
Softly in my ear
For it is one of the most beautiful times
Of the year

When squirrels gather acorns
And nuts on the ground
When colorful leaves fall downward
Without ever making a sound

Soon a cold wind will be blowing
And a frosty morn will chill my face
Soon the leaves will be gone
As winter takes autumn's place

God made the seasons
And autumn is a favorite one for me
Yes, as I gaze at all the colors
I'm happy as can be

Christmas

May the joy of Christmas come your way
For the Christ child was born of Christmas day

The angels sang, giving God glory above
For God had sent down his everlasting love

The shepherds were filled with wonder and joy
Mary watched, as they worshiped her baby boy

A bright star shined over the manger that night
And kings from afar saw this great light

These wise men came and gifts each gave
Worshiping the Lord, who has the power to save

This baby Jesus was destined to hang on Calvary
For the sins of you and me

Yes, God's son was born on Christmas night
Bringing hope to the world and providing them light

Who Said Its Winter

Who said its winter
Jack Frost says its so
He shows up in the morning
And I think he should know

And my grass says its winter
Its color is an awful brown
Yes, it's just waiting for springtime
And redbreast robins to come around

And I also say its winter
Yes, I often feel its chilly air
Especially when I walk my dog Lucy
And the cold wind blows my face and hair

But I thank God for winter
Also spring, summer, and autumn too
I also thank him for Jesus
And his love for me and you

Who else says its winter
Well God says its so
He's the one who created everything
Yes, even the frost, the sleet, and the snow

Looking Ahead With Great Expectations

The year two thousand fourteen
Has opened its doors wide
And all of earth's inhabitants
Have entered inside

And although no one knows
What two thousand fourteen will bring
Remember God is still in control
Of everything

So let's not be found with fear
As we enter this New Year

For our fate is truly in God's wonderful hands
And who can defer what he chooses or plans

He's the Lord of heaven and earth
And the creator of you and me
Nothing can happen this year
Unless he allows those events to be

And so this year let's reverence him
And Jesus Christ his son
While looking ahead with great expectations
And praying that his will, will be done

The Spirit of Giving

We celebrate Christmas in many ways
For it's a very special time of year
To enjoy the holidays

To some Christmas is quite holy
A time to turn to God and pray
And offer good will to everyone
Because Christ was born on Christmas day

But to others it may be about Santa
And gifts under the Christmas tree
There may be no mention of Christ's birth
Or how he died to set men free

But however one celebrates,
Let's try not to fuss
Let's just try to remember
That Christ is God's gift to us

Also while we're in the spirit of giving
If we remember those who are in need
Then we'll receive blessings from Heaven
For God sees every good deed

The New Year

It's goodbye to the old year
And a big welcome to the new
As the last sand in the hourglass
Helps us reminisce the year we've been thru

And as we reminisce
Let's thank God for the past year
For from him came our blessings
And everything else we hold dear

Also let's make new years resolutions,
Then speak them softly into God's ear
Then keep them faithfully
All thru the coming New Year

And also to our friends and neighbors,
Let's resolve that when we see them in need,
That we'll be there beside them
Both in spirit and in deed

Then the New Year will have more meaning
And bring us excitement every day
For whenever we chose to help others
God always provides us a way

Our Moms

Our moms can be good
Our moms can be bad
As I reminisce oe'r the past
I love the mom I had

She held me as a babe
Yes, I nursed upon her breast
Then she sang me a lullaby
Then off to sleep I'd rest

As I grew and learned to walk
I seldom felt mom's wrath
For she was always there for me
To gently guide me down --- life's path

She took all of us children
To church on Sunday morn
Then prayed a seed of faith
In each of us would be born

A wise son heareth his father's
Instruction Proverbs 13:1

Father's Day

We call them father, papa and even dad
But when they take us in their arms
We feel so glad

My dad worked hard to make ends meet
Yes, raising seven children was an awesome feat

He taught us to respect others
As we went on our way
Yes, "Stay out of trouble,"
Is what he would often say

Later on in life
He read the bible every day
And come Sunday morning
It was off to church to worship and to pray

We were so sad
When his life came to an end
But he had a good life
And that's quite a message to send

So while we celebrate Fathers Day
I'll remember dad
And all the good things he had to say

The Seasons Come And Go

Spring suddenly comes
Then summer takes its place
Then autumn's colors come along
Before winter's chill hits our face

And so it is
The seasons come and go
And then one day it happens
Our age begins to show

For we're only here on this earth
Just a little while
Then it will be over
Yes, we'll travel our last mile

But before we die and leave this earth
Yes, on this very day
Could we thank God for his goodness
Before we continue on our way

For he sent his only son Jesus
To die on Calvary's tree
That all who would trust in him
Would be pardoned and set free

Yes, the seasons come and go
The years quickly pass by
But if we place our trust and faith in Jesus
We'll go to heaven when we die

You'll Never Be The Same

Are you searching for answers
Does life seem like a dead end
Do you feel there's no hope for tomorrow
And you need a close friend

Then turn to the Lord Jesus
And invite him to come in
Your life will be changed
And he'll forgive you of your sins

Then you'll receive hope for tomorrow
And strength for today
As your faith increases
He'll guide your way

Also he'll never disappoint you
Neither lead you down the wrong road
He has all the answers
And he'll lighten your load

So trust him today
You'll never be the same
One day he'll introduce you
To his heavenly father
And give you a new name

CPSIA information can be obtained at www.ICGtesting.com
Printed in the USA
LVOW07s0857140415

434436LV00001B/15/P